THINGS THAT URINATE ME OFF!!!

Christopher Slough
Things That Urinate Me Off!!!

Published by BooxAi

ISBN: 978-965-578-100-7

THINGS THAT URINATE ME OFF!!!

PET PEEVES OF A SOUTH TEXAS COWBOY

CHRIS SLOUGH

ASSOCIATED EDITOR
RACHELLE WATERS

COVER ILLUSTRATION BY
COURTNEY FAISON GRASTY

Dedicated to my Cousin/Brother, Sid Smith and my friend Glenn Hyden who coined the phrase: "that urinates me off."

CONTENTS

PREFACE

For those of you who read my book, do so with an open mind and a sense of humor.

If you are opposed to differing ideas, don't read it! If an occasional cuss word bothers you, don't read it!

I don't pull punches, and I pick on everyone.

I am 66 years old and I don't give a big rat's ass if I offend your insecure sensibilities!

I am a former bull rider, bull dogger, cop, fireman, medic, barber, business owner, musician, singer and flight attendant. As well as husband (times 3) father, grandfather and die-hard Texan and die-hard American.

Enjoy!

CHAPTER 1
RELIGION

I want to get this crap out of the way. In this chapter, I'm sure I will urinate off atheists and agnostics alike with my opinions, but fear not! I know for a fact that I will urinate folks of faith off as well!

I am a Christian. Not a good one, if there is such a thing.

I know all the atheists and agnostics out there, regard folks like me as being ignorant, anti-science, closed-minded, judgmental believers of a big fairy tale and hoax. Hmmm?

That sounds pretty freaking judgmental and closed-minded to me! It amazes me that non-believers cannot just respect us for the beliefs we choose and live their own lives. They constantly try to demean us and make us out to be less intelligent than they!

On the other side of that coin, it amazes me that self-righteous bible thumpers are far more judgmental of folks of faith who do not adopt all their beliefs as their own than they are of atheists who regard them as idiots.

I chose years ago to believe that Jesus is the son of God. I choose to believe that when he was crucified for heresy, which is a historical fact, he rose from death and is my savior.

I've witnessed too many occurrences and sheer miracles that could not be explained away with science to deny the existence of a higher power. I call it God!

I choose the teaching of Jesus because he is the only religious figure who taught unconditional love and forgiveness.

Do I believe my faith is the only way to know God? Hell NO!

I believe God loves us all, and it is not my place to judge anyone. I am only commanded by God to love ALL of his children, and I do.

I love you until you force me not to!

I will love you and help you no matter what your beliefs, ethnicity, gender, size, weight, sexual orientation or political leanings may be.

Now, I'm going to urinate many believers off, if I haven't already.

Do I believe the Bible is infallible? No! It was written hundreds of years after Jesus' death and resurrection by a bunch of theologists (all male) who, though inspired by God, were mere men.

These men would oppress women for thousands of years and still do, even though Jesus exalted women throughout the New Testament!

It has been rewritten hundreds of times. Do I think the New Testament is infallible? No! Again, it was written by mere men. I have studied the teachings of Mathew, Mark, Luke and John and I have chosen to keep my beliefs deeply rooted in these teachings, which chronicle Jesus' journey on Earth and all of the miracles he performed along with his love and ultimate sacrifice for mankind.

As far as the Old Testament goes, I use it only as a historical reference filled with teachings and stories that use symbolic events and characters to illustrate God's plan.

Back to atheists and agnostics – I know you are now thinking I am ignorant and do not believe in science. Sorry guys, but you are wrong. I am amazed, and I marvel at all of the scientific occurrences and discoveries which have occurred even in my lifetime.

How can I believe in science and in God? In case you haven't heard, one of the most famous scientists and smartest men who ever lived believed that in his study of science he came to realize that there must be a higher power who designed the universe. That scientist was Albert Einstein. I won't quote him and let you pick me apart. I'll refer you to one of the smartest men on the planet today; Michio Kaku. In his book "The God Equation" he tells of his goal of proving Einstein's theory of the existence of God.

My belief is that God was always there. I also believe in the enormity of God's power and glory.

I believe that God used every theory of science in existence and many we have not yet discovered. After all, He created the universe.

Because of his power and glory, I believe he (or she, or it) used the Big Bang in an enormous explosion of color to begin. Then, I believe he used everything from primordial soup to evolution to continue in the creation. I find it very sad that science-minded folks often keep their minds closed off to the possibility of God's existence. Science should be the most open-minded thing there is. To quote the Bible – "With God, all things are possible."

Two examples of why I don't take the Bible verbatim:

How often have you heard that Eve committed the first sin? Wrong! When God created Eve as a helpmate and wife to Adam, he commanded Adam to be the spiritual leader, provider and protector of his family. Not the head or the boss.

When Eve was first tempted (not a sin), Adam was not there. He was goofing off in the garden somewhere! When Eve took him to the forbidden fruit tree, he should have been the spiritual leader, provider and protector of his family.

Had he been the protector, he would have cut the head off the serpent and then he would have taken Eve to safety. Teaching her to trust God and obey God's one rule – to avoid the forbidden fruit.

Also, when Adam and Eve became embarrassed by their sin, what did God say?

He said "Adam! Where are you?" which shows his disappointment in Adam!

Therefore, Adam committed the first sin.

How many times have you heard that "Money is the root of all evil."? Wrong! It is "The love of money that is the root of all evil!". When money becomes your God, it becomes evil.

Okay. Enough of religion! Let's go to politics so I can really urinate some folks on both sides of the aisle off!

But, first, I want to say that I find it sad that folks can't see the beauty and the beautiful faces of our children and do not believe that there must be something beyond this life.

CHAPTER 2
POLITICS

First of all – I am a "centrist", libertarian, independent or whatever label you want to stick on me.

In regard to government, I lean right. I want the government to be small and leave me the hell alone! As far as helping those less fortunate, I lean toward common-sense solutions. I want the government to keep our borders secure, unlike the Buffoon Biden plan. Also, protect us from foreign invaders, or we will protect ourselves. Watch the movie "Red Dawn" (Patrick Swayze). I want other countries to treat us fairly in trade and commerce. I know you left-leaning liberals hate Trump, but he renegotiated trade agreements to our advantage, unlike Buffoon Biden. Trump is an egotistical ass, but he put America First, as any leader should!

We went from Obama's $3.00 gas to $1.75, with almost no inflation and a high GDP. Stocks up and unemployment down for all groups. He was working on getting more industry to return to the USA. I hope we get him back before Biden destroys us.

Okay – I know liberals hate me now, but hang with me. I'm going to blast both democrats and republicans alike.

Democrats: Party of big government, big spending, anti-police and military. They try to destroy opponents not by policies but by defamation and character assassination. They condemn patriots of either party as domestic terrorists. They want to disarm us all, so they can take us over.

They support Marxist groups that loot and pillage cities. They support Woke ideas. They have exploited climate change and are destroying our economy with their Green New Deal which is a stupid name. New Green Deal would at least be grammatically correct.

Finally, they never put America first.

Republicans: Too many rhino republicans like McConnel, Cheney and others claim to be fiscally conservative while voting for big spending efforts. They talk a good game but play another.

Basically, both parties suck and it urinates me off to no end that these jerks are in control.

CHAPTER 3
ABORTION

Now I'm going to tackle the gorilla in the room: Abortion.

Now I'll urinate both sides off.

Extreme democrats support abortion with little or no limits. They want me to pay for other people's choices of abortion. Hell no! I have no problem providing free contraceptives, but I personally do not want to fund abortions.

Republicans use abortion to appease the far right-wing evangelicals. You know those Godly folks who don't give a shit about the plight of these girls. These folks are pro-birth, not pro -life! Ask them to take a girl into their home, take care of her, and when the baby is born, adopt the baby and raise the child as their own. Like that would ever happen!

If you aren't willing to be part of the solution, shut the hell up about the problem.

Problem 1

The overturning of Roe v Wade opened the door to right-wing nut jobs passing laws the make abortion illegal past six weeks, as in my state, Texas.

Many women don't know they are pregnant by then, and it makes risky pregnancies and ectopic pregnancies illegal to deal with. At least most states are saying 15 weeks and are making exceptions for risky situations. You know – Common Sense!!!

I just pray that someone in my state will grow a damn brain!

I am pro-choice with a caveat. If you choose to kill the being growing inside you for whatever reason, make your damn decision and do it within the first trimester!

Problem 2

Our government needs to get high-dollar attorneys out of the adoption process. Make it easier to adopt here than in China.

It is ridiculous that you can fly to China and adopt a child for half of what it costs to adopt in American child with less red tape.

And in the immortal words of Forest Gump: "That's all I have to say about that."

CHAPTER 4
GOVERNMENT THIEVERY

We need a constitutional amendment outlawing the use of ear marks and coat tail shenanigans. Also, outlawing the merging of two unrelated items on one bill and lobbying payoffs as treason.

Also, make it as an act of treason to charge more for goods, services or construction in government contracts than you would to the general public.

Give government folks and departments rules that save money. No more – "If you don't spend your yearly allotment, you'll lose it bullshit. Finally, bring in term limits across the board. And make it to that any congressional pay hikes must be voted in on election day. Even past that, put limits and boundaries on congressional trips! No private jets. Congressmen can fly commercially. Rand Paul flies commercial. I've had him on my plane and he is awesome!

Destroy inherent corruption!

CHAPTER 5
CRIMINALS

I believe all violent acts must be met with stiff prison terms and in many cases, death. Limit appeals on smoking gun cases. Now is when I'll urinate folks off. I do not believe non-violent criminals should go to prison. Shut up and listen! Common theft and white-collar thieves should be forced to work and pay 25% of their salary to their victims. Bernie Madoff should have been forced to use his knowledge to make some of the millions back for his victims rather than sit in federal prison. If they don't have a job, put their asses to work on the roads, bridges, helping the elderly with house repairs or their yards. Pay them $3,000 per month instead of paying $80,000 per year per inmate. Have them pay 25% of their earnings to their victims and if it was a victimless crime, have them give 25% to programs to help less fortunate folks,

Incarceration was utterly stupid for a kid with a bag of weed. It is ludicrous! When we as cops had to waste time on pot, it opened the door to the drugs like cocaine, LSD, PCP and now Fentanyl. Another thing – make prison hard. Bring back chain gangs. Have them work in the prison farm.

Feed them cold cereal for breakfast, a bologna sandwich for lunch and one hot meal a day. If it's good enough for kids and soldiers, it's good enough for them.

Therefore: Adopt Sheriff Arpaio's method. The prisoners wear pink jumpsuits with rubber flip-flops or running shoes. They do daily calisthenics, no bar bells, no tattoos given in prison, no porn, violent books or movies. Forced counselling and educational programs for carpentry, plumbing, etc. No law degrees, not free elective surgeries, or elective dental work. Only necessary health care, you know, like what we working folks have. I also believe that conjugal visits should never be allowed. Prison should be punishment.

Folks who get arrested for a DUI and who did not have an accident hurting anyone shouldn't be put in jail. Let them have the blower installed in their car so they can go to work. Taking away their ability to drive to work makes no sense!

Turn the thousands of empty prisons into homeless shelters, animal shelters and, my favorite – veteran housing!

Can anyone tell me why these ideas won't work?

This is a biggie for me. I am so urinated off by this liberal, left-wing "soft on crime" liberal D.A.s who are releasing violent criminals on their own recognizance. What the "F—k" is this? In New York, a convicted criminal, who has been arrested eighteen times, used a lead-lined glove, came up behind a young man and hammered him into the ground, fracturing his skull, breaking his jaw and leaving him in a fight for his life. The New York D.A. let him out two hours after his arrest. New York is turning into a shit hole run by who? Democrats! LA, Chicago, Portland, San Francisco, Seattle and Philly have become crime-riddled, homeless-invaded shitholes, all run by who? Democrats!

If you criminals ever make the mistake of entering my home, don't feel confident that liberal catch-and-release policies with save you! I will send you right to hell!

I have my own policy. Bag and bury!

If you threaten my family, I'll kill your ass graveyard dead, and there won't even be any DNA left. "Bless your heart". For those of you who are non-Texans, that means F__k yourself!

CHAPTER 6
COVID AND CANCER

In recent years I've learned that there are two health issues I've come to hate:

Covid, as it turns out, is a man-made virus that I believe was unleashed upon the world population as folks like Bill Gates and Dr. Fauci stated was needed seven years ago. It also served another purpose. It was exploited to the degree that certain corporations like Pfizer, Johnson & Johnson, Moderna, Walmart, Home Depot, Lowes and others made billions while controlling the population with lockdowns and forcing small businesses to close. Also, the socialist Democratic left wing got another prize. Because Trump trusted the CDC and Fauci, who initially told him it would be mild and short-lived. He couldn't stay off Twitter, he lost the 2020 election, which saddled America with Buffoon Biden and more radical left-wingers pushing their Green New Deal. However, the worst thing about Covid that urinated me off to an almost impossible degree, was that it took the life of my cousin Sid. He and I were in the process of taking over a security company in San Antonio, Texas and buying a gorgeous ranch in Bandera, Texas. He, my wife

Rachelle and I were going to live on the ranch like Three's Company. I'm still broken inside, but I'm coming through it. Rachelle has helped me get it back together. As I see it, Fauci, the FDA and the CDC murdered my cousin Sid. Oh, and I refuse to call Fauci a doctor. That son of a bitch killed Sid and millions of others around the world.

Cancer has been my nemesis since 2005. While going through a divorce, I came down with colon cancer. I had the surgery and started chemo. In 2006 it went to my liver. I was given two years to live. Many more surgeries, chemo and radiation later, I'm still here!

I went into full remission in 2010. In 2017 I married Rachelle and after the honeymoon, we went to my doctor in Dallas only to find that though I had beaten colon and stage 4 liver cancer, I had kidney cancer. They took my left kidney and I was good!

Last year I was diagnosed with breast cancer and had a mastectomy. Breast cancer kills most male victims because men are inherently stupid. Instead of checking out the lump, most of them would have ignored it. I'll expound on that in my "Men urinate me off" chapter.

I started getting worried about my future in the breathing department. Finally, I decided that if cancer was going to kill me, that son of a bitch was gonna damn sure know he's been in a fight! One last point: if the FDA and CDC really don't give a Tinker's Damn about us, why did they block the use of Ivermectin and Hydrochloraquine for treating Covid?! Now it is widely used. Why have they not outlawed the use of Aspartame in our food? It is one of the most carcinogenic substances known to man!

Screw Covid

Screw Cancer

Screw the CDC

Screw Fauci

Screw the FDA

I thank God for Dr. Brooks and Dr. Gogel every day. When someone asks "How are you today?" I say "I'm doing great! I got up this morning, everything works pretty well and I'm on top of the dirt. Everything else will work itself out. If you ever wake up and see roots above you, it's not a good day. Then I say "Hell can't handle me, Heaven ain't ready for me and God's not gonna put up with my ass until he has to!".

CHAPTER 7
MEN

Now that I have insulted men in the previous chapter, I'm going to keep on.

Men urinate me off so badly that I want to kick their asses and say "Straighten the hell up!"

#1 Be a gentleman!!!

#2 Be honest!

#3 Be dependable!

#4 Be loyal!

#5 Be a protector

#6 Be compassionate

#7 Be loving

What really urinates me off is men who fall short of these seven easy principles.

7 deadly sins by men:

#1 Abusiveness

#2 Violence

#3 Emotional bullying

#4 Neglectfulness

#5 Being conniving

#6 Cheating

#7 Manipulativeness

To quote my wife's good friend Monty – "Why do women like us? We're disgusting!".

Men are inherently stupid. I, myself, have done many stupid things.

CHAPTER 8
WOMEN

What can I say about women? Women are God's answer to the mistakes he made in men. It's good that he made women take care of men, because we are too stupid to take care of ourselves. Case in point: Have you ever seen pics on Facebook of the guy 25 feet in the air on a 2x4 stud balanced on two extension ladders? I rest my case.

However, women do a few things that totally urinate me off.

First of all, I, and many other men, were taught to be gentlemen. When we hold a door open or offer to carry you over a water puddle, we are not saying you can't handle it. We are merely trying to brighten your day and make you feel special. Please let us be the gentlemen we were taught to be.

Another thing that women do that almost makes me want to wear Depends. It urinates me off so much. I see so many times that a woman will be dating a guy who treats her like a queen and will dump him for what they see as a cool Billy Badass, who will inevitably show his true colors. Once she invites him into her life, he becomes abusive and manipulative. There are the seven rules for being a great woman:

#1 Love and respect yourself

#2 Never live with or marry an abusive man. He will not change!

#3 Realize that men act tough, but we are actually big babies.

#4 Coddle us for about ten minutes, then tell us to get off our asses and be real men.

#5 Please allow us to be romantic. We try and sometimes succeed!

#6 Love us with your whole soul.

#7 Be the woman God created you to be.

Interjection:

Okay – I know you are getting bored with all my philosophical rantings, so I'm going to address a subject that will make some of you explode!

CHAPTER 9
WOKE-ISM

Woke-ism!!!

See? You are already urinated off, and I haven't even spoken.

First of all, I don't have anything against members of our LGTBQ gender-neutral community, so shut the hell up and listen! Would you like to know why folks are resistant to think about or address your concerns?

Well, first of all, it is your terminology.

Woke sounds stupid!

Awakened would be much better (and grammatically correct),

If you don't want to be called he or she, that's fine! However, 'them' and 'they' are plural words. One person cannot be a "they" unless they are schizophrenic! In other words, multiple personalities. It just sounds ignorantly stupid and grammatically horrid! Also, don't assume that I, being a 66 year old white man, am phobic, racist, sexist or any other "ist" toward you. You don't like being stereotyped and stuck with labels. Neither do I!

However, when you call yourself them or they, you have just labeled yourselves.

Look, I don't have anything against you for your choices. However, what urinates me off is your branding of non-woke folks as ignorant, homophobic, oppressors of the LGBTQRSTPieRsquare community. I don't give a flip what you do. Just don't push your "Woke" bullshit on me.

By the way, there are only two genders. Scientifically your DNA is either male or female. Even with a sex change operation, your DNA will stay the same, either XX or XY. Period.

If you want to be respected, change your terminology and admit that this multiple-gender stuff is your emotional choice, not a scientific fact.

CHAPTER 10
RACISM

I am a 66 year old white guy, so I have to be a racist. This urinates me off to no end. I have never in my life treated anyone differently because of the color of their skin, their social standing, their looks, their education level, their political or religious beliefs, or their sexual orientation. But many folks automatically brand me as a racist. Period!

CHAPTER 11
EDUCATORS

First of all, I have great respect for dedicated teachers. However, it thoroughly urinates me off when I see elementary kids taught gender reassignment and being taught by drag queens. Let kids be kids. Let them believe in Sant Claus and the Easter Bunny. Let them play tag and hide and seek!

Teach them reading, writing, arithmetic, science, history, geography, computer skills and life skills. For example, home economics, general business, shop, agriculture, etc. In other words, teach them to be successful in life. Not to question their gender identities.

Let kids be kids!!!

CHAPTER 12
WOKE CORPORATIONS

One thing that really urinates me off is the woke policies being adopted by American corporations. These policies label their white employees as racist. They force their workers to attend seminars that show white heterosexual workers as racist, homophobic, anti-minority bigots who oppress all not-white workers. These corporations spy on workers' Facebook and Twitter feeds, searching for every chance to find reasons to fire them. If these policies were fair and equitable to all workers, I'd have no problem with them. However, the fact is that in many cases, these corporations conveniently only find fire-able posts on white employee feeds. In many cases, these corporations never find fire-able posts by minorities, which means they are exempt from being called racist.

It has become today's version of Affirmative Action.

CHAPTER 13
DRIVERS

Learn how to freakin drive! Watch out for motorcycles.

Dos: Pay attention,

Follow the flow of traffic,

The fast lane is for fast,

The slow lane is for slow.

Leave enough space between you and the next car.

Don'ts

Don't drive in others' blind spots.

Don't drink and drive.

Don't text and drive.

Don't kill me on my bike,

Don't assume that I see you.

My wife says I have a serious road rage problem, so don't urinate me off!

. . .

Finally – stay the hell out of my way!

Just like every other driver, I am the only good driver on the road. Stay safe out there!

CHAPTER 14
BE NICE!

It really urinates me off to a catastrophic level forcing me to consider wearing depends when I see people exploding with anger, myself included, over everyday problems, disagreements and situations.

When I was in a supervisory role and my employees would have conflicts in which they yelled and screamed at each other, I would say "Shut up, or you are fired!" Then, after they called down, I would say I have one rule – Be Nice!!!

I can fix any problem if we are nice. This is true in business, parenting and friendships.

Food for thought.

CHAPTER 15
CLIMATE CHANGE

I really get urinated off at all the folks who have bought into this.

Climate change has been around since the dawn of time. Weather has changed throughout many cycles. It amazes me that climate folks believe anything that folks like Al Gore and John Kerry say, even though their personal habits include flying in gas-guzzling smog and carbon-belching private jets while telling us to take the bus. I'm an old guy and I remember all of the claims since the 60s.

In the 60's, we were told oil would be depleted in ten years. Didn't happen.

In the 70's we were told that we were destined for an Ice Age. Didn't happen.

In the 80's we were told that acid rain would kill us all. Didn't happen. Environmental efforts fixed this, not added taxes and exploitation. The world came together with common sense solutions laid out. By the 1987 Montreal Protocol, which was signed by 197 countries.

In the 90's we were told the Ozone layer would die, killing us with the sun's heat and radiation. Didn't happen. Environmental efforts fixed this. Not added taxes and exploitation! The world came together with common sense solutions laid out by the 1987 Montreal Protocol, which was signed by 197 countries. The first treaty in the history of the United Nations to achieve universal ratification, and it is considered by many the most successful environmental global action.

In the 2000's we were told that multiple types of climate changes are causing icebergs to melt, raising sea levels to dangerous levels. Didn't happen.

We have been told that Polar Bears are going extinct. They're not. In the 90's, Polar Bears numbered less than 10 thousand. Today, they number over 30,000, as per the discovery channel.

The amazing thing is that every one of these claims resulted in higher taxes and exploiters like Kerry and Gore becoming billionaires. Oh! And Americans are saddled with 90% of the world with the cost of this lunacy. They say if we older guys had recycled, we wouldn't have these problems. Hmmm? We used reusable glass bottles for everything from bleach to milk to cokes.

For you young ones filling our landfills and ocean with plastic water bottles – Kiss my old wrinkled-up ass!

CHAPTER 16
ELECTRIC CARS

Okay, all of these climate alarmists keep saying to get electric cars to save the environment. Evidently, they've never seen a lithium or cobalt mine. They strip mines for miles on earth, destroying the soil for decades. The batteries are not recyclable and the electric cars are extremely expensive for something you can only go 250 miles before you they need to be recharged.

Elon Musk said he is working toward a balance of fossil fuels and electric vehicles that are going to be necessary for many, many years. Accept it and move on!

If you want to buy an overpriced electric car, knock yourself out, but don't try to bullshit me with your "Green New Deal" propaganda.

It urinates me off to no end! There are not any parts of these cars that are green.

These cars are built by factories which operate with fossil fuels!

I see where California is outlawing the sale of fossil fuel run cars by 2035. California is already having rolling brownouts and blackouts, and they really think their electrical grid can withstand millions of electric cars drawing from it.

CHAPTER 17
WIND GENERATORS AND SOLAR PANELS

I'm not against either, but don't say they are "green". Wind generators use up to 1000 gallons of oil per year per generator. The blades are fiberglass and cannot be recycled. They only last up to two years and then they are buried in landfills.

The vast majority of solar panels are made in China thanks to the Obama/Biden love affair with the Chinese Communists. This Green New Deal Biden and AOC have forced on us will possibly destroy our economy. Its name even sounds stupid. The New Green Deal would at least be grammatically correct of course, it was named by a party girl barback who couldn't hold a job until the idiot New York liberal left-wing nut jobs elected her to congress.

CHAPTER 18
STUDENT LOANS

Oh my God! We constantly hear about the plight of young folks not paying their student loans and wanting the government to forgive them by cancelling their debt.

First of all, like all loans, you agree to pay them back. If you are borrowing $200,000, you might consider choosing a field of study that actually has a career plan that will pay you enough to live and pay your loan back. I'm sorry, but a degree in women's studies, African studies or underwater basket weaving will never pay a decent wage. At best, they will get you a sales job. One of the problems is that counselors in high school and college do a piss poor job of directing students, because they have to push so many students to these obscure lesson plans to justify keeping professors in the classroom, not train the kids.

In Buffoon Biden's plan, he wants to forgive all student loans but immediately make these folks eligible to borrow more money, and he claims it will not raise taxes or inflation. What a freaking idiot!!!

Oh, but wait! Life, now, is so hard. Bull shit.

My parents and grandparents went through the damn Great Depression and survived with no help from the government. In my own life, there were many times that I worked three different jobs to feed my family without a 1000 dollar cell phone and tattoos, so cry me a f__king river!

I don't mind if they lower interest rates or even eliminate them, but I don't want my tax dollars to bail them out. How about making colleges roll back prices? It's amazing that up until Buffoon Biden policies, inflation was less than 3% since 2000. Why is it that colleges and universities raise their prices by 30 – 40% every year? Because, with government-backed loans and no limits or regulations aimed at institutions of higher learning, these folks have screwed college kids for decades.

Case in point. My sister went to the University of Texas in Tyler. She earned her bachelors. She had applied for a grant, but decided not to use it. The money never went to her from UT Tyler, but they are holding her transcript even though the grant was never used. This is criminal. What makes it even sadder is that the majority of colleges are run by left-wing nutjobs who squelch differing opinions. If a student is conservative, he or she must hide it if they are to get good grades. Conservative speakers are booed off the stage because these leftist professors are indoctrinating kids to hate American capitalism and adopt socialism. Bottom line is that, as in all areas of finance, if you willingly take out a loan, you are expected to pay it back. Period!!!

CHAPTER 19
FOREIGNERS PURCHASING BUSINESSES, LAND AND REAL ESTATE

China is buying up all of the real estate and farmland it can get its hands on. Funny how much of it is near military bases.

Funny how liberal Democrats and Rhino Republicans don't see that as a threat. They can eventually control our food supply and plant insurgents and arms near our bates. In Switzerland and many other countries, in order to buy property or businesses, you must have a Swiss partner. One of the reasons, along with a well-armed citizenry, that nobody screws with the Swiss. The problem is that we allow foreigners to make campaign contributions and lobby for their interests. How stupid has America become? As I said before, Trump may be a big asshole, but at least he tried to put America first, unlike China Joe and his meth-head son. Keep America for Americans.

CHAPTER 20
CHINA

Speaking of China Joe

How about our Southern border, Joe? What a fiasco!

Trump had our border secure and was building the wall when China Joe came in. He opened the border allowing over four million illegals to cross our border, bringing crime, disease and Fentanyl. It also caused spikes in human and sex trafficking. All of this in a year and a half. Then, he put Kamala Harris in charge. How many trips to the border has this waste of skin and bone made? None!

She's the most worthless VP in history. Of course, Buffoon Biden is the worst president in history. Not just poor Mexicans seeking a better life are crossing. Middle Eastern men, (some who are on the terror watch list), and folks from all over with no vetting are given a cell phone, money and supplies and a plane ticket!

The Fentanyl crisis is mind-boggling. Since idiot Joe opened the floodgates on day one, death from drugs has gone up way over 100,000 per year, and over 70% were involving Fentanyl.

Now it's coming in rainbow colors like Capt. Crunch Marshmallows to target kids. Thanks Joe! This idiot has placed us all at risk. Now before the mid-term election, he's haphazardly building part of Trump's wall to buy votes. What a piece of human garbage. Buffoon Biden is the proper face of the Democratic Socialist party. They have never done anything for the ethnic and socio-economic groups they have exploited for so long. Every time I see Biden's face, it urinates me off to no end that all these educated liberals have saddled America with this racist, communist idiot.

CHAPTER 21
FLAG KNEELERS

To all the pro athletes kneeling for the national anthem, To Hell with you. If you want to fight to get rid of bad police officers, work with civic leaders in a positive way. Don't spit in the face of every man and woman who fought and in many cases, died for your freedom. LeBron James claims he's treated like a slave. I had never heard of a slave making 20 million a year. This Brittney Griner idiot who wouldn't come out of the locker room for the anthem went to Russia with drugs. She got caught and was sentenced to nine years. Now, this America hater wants America to bail her ass out, and Biden plans to trade a Russian terrorist arms dealer for her, putting the world in danger. Screw her. Let her play basketball for the Russian prison system.

Our country has had dark days, but we came out of them. We still have more to do, but this is the greatest county on earth, Buffoon Biden and the democratic socialists are trying like hell to destroy it, so they can get us under a world government with the Clintons, Bushes, Obamas, Bidens and Soros at the helm.

I love my country and I will fight to the death to protect it.

If you want socialism, move to Venezuela. Bottom line is that if you don't love America, get the Hell out!

CHAPTER 22
GUN CONTROL

For all of you anti-gun folks: if you want an unarmed society, move! We will not give up our guns. Period!

Beto can spout out all he wants about taking our guns, but he doesn't have the guts to try to actually take them. We don't give a rip what any of you think, the second amendment guarantees our right to be armed! Read it and weep bitches! You want to disarm legal gun owners, but not one of you bastards talks of disarming criminals.

So kiss my old white wrinkled-up ass!

CHAPTER 23
RAISING YOUR KIDS

Before I begin, I want to admit – I was a mediocre father. Through my bad habits, I caused my kids to have to deal with weight problems. I didn't take care of their dental issues as I should have. I was just an okay dad.

However, my kids never felt unloved. They all knew I would kill or die for them. I still would today. If you f__k with my wife, her family, my parents, sister, kids, grandkids, cousins, friends, or my country, I will kill your ass graveyard dead. And there won't even be any DNA left, so you better pray to your God, if you believe in one, that the cops get your ass before I do.

Seven rules for good parenting of your children:

#1 Love them more than life itself

#2 Teach them to love and respect themselves

#3 Pay attention to what they are being taught in school, church or organizations

#4 Teach you boys to be gentlemen and your girls to never accept any man who is not!

#5 Always be honest with your kids

#6 Be willing to kill or die for them

#7 Listen with your ears and your heart. They may be crying for help

One last thing. When your school board member, teacher, unions, college professors and your government call you terrorists for monitoring your kid's education, vote the bastards out! Never allow this new bunch of Woke, indoctrinating socialists to influence your kids toward beliefs that contradict your values, but, at the same time, never squelch your child's imagination and curiosity to learn other things.

Also, teach your children to love and respect people of all walks of life. Teach them to be kind, to love, to laugh and to live.

Remember, you can live to die or you can live to live.

CHAPTER 24
ATTITUDES

Be nice and think positive. I know we all have moments when things just are not the way we want them to be, but we try to keep positive. Blow off some steam and then snap out of it.

Positive attitudes breed positive results. Negative attitudes breed negative results. Plus, no one likes a curmudgeon. We all have sad stories. We've all lost loved ones. Many of us have had catastrophic injuries or illnesses. We've had money problems. We all got through bad things. What defines us is how we work through these events, and how we prepare so that we don't make the same mistakes!

I have battled colon, stage four liver, kidney and breast cancer since 2005 and I could have rolled up like a doodlebug, but I am a survivor, and when I was told I had a couple of years to live, I said cancer may kill me, but that bastard will damn sure know he's been in a fight. I'll fight that SOB to my last breath!

There was a singer on America's Got Talent with terminal cancer called

Night Bird who had a sweet spirit and said "You can't wait for life to be easy before you decide to be happy."

She passed away and I know that heaven's light was brighter that day.

God bless Night Bird. If she could have such a sweet spirit in her condition, what the hell are we bitching about?

CHAPTER 25
RUDE PEOPLE

Like I said earlier: Be Nice!

I see so many folks barging in front of people to get somewhere. If you are in that big of a hurry, leave earlier!

Rude drivers cut people off, putting everyone in danger. Watch your foul language. On my airplane, guys come in spouting the F word right in front of little kids, families and even nuns!

You show your lack of intelligence. Also, for all of you young guys with your pants on your ass – pull your damn pants UP!

You don't look cool or tough. You look like a "Prison Bitch".

That shit began back in the 20's. Weak cons had their pants low to advertise that they were bitches to the tough guys, so instead of looking like a badass, you look like a free piece of ass. Bah Hah! I crack myself up!

When folks at the store leave their baskets out in the parking lot, I want to ram that cart into the side of their car. Put it in the rack, or take it back to the store. And, for all of you who through dirty diapers in the parking lot, carry a f__king trash bag. It totally urinates me off when I see folks throw trash on the lot when there is a trash can 20 feet away. If you do that shit in front of me, I'll throw it in, or on your car!

When you get stopped by a cop, shut the hell up! Get your license and insurance out. Keep your smart-ass mouth shut and your hands in plain sight. If you do that, you will not get shot!

When I was a cop, I stopped a guy just to tell him that his tail Lights were flickering and he probably had a short. He jumped out of his car and hit me. After I put his ass on the ground in handcuffs, he apologized, stating that he had caught his wife in bed with his best friend.

I could have charged him with felony assault of a peace officer, but instead, I took him across the street to my favorite Mexican food restaurant, had dinner, talked with him and calmed him down. The fact is, you don't know why you are being stopped. Don't jump out cussing and yelling racism when you have no clue why he stopped you. Being nice and polite will get you better results no matter what the situation may be.

CHAPTER 26
MOVIE THEATERS

It's no wonder you are all going broke. With all the streaming services, you guys are still raping the public like you did before HBO and Blockbuster! $12-15 to get in, $7 cokes, $12 popcorn and $10 hot dogs. Maybe drive-ins will make a resurgence. Well, I guess if you morons don't grow some cranial matter that actually works, we can turn all of the empty theaters into homeless shelters.

CHAPTER 27
MOVIES AND SPORTS

I am so tired of movie critics and the Oscars bad-mouthing movies people actually go to see, and giving awards to activist movies based on race or gender.

Case in point; a few years ago, La La Land, a box office smash, was beaten for Best Picture by an activist movie, Moonlight, a movie that didn't draw anywhere close to what La La Land drew. It seems the Hollywood elites are only going to vote for a movie pushing certain agendas.

Another thing that totally urinates me off is the fact that professional sports have become unaffordable to the common family. With $300 plus tickets and $10 hotdogs, taking an average family of four can cost as much as 1,000 dollars or more.

It is ridiculous when teams pay these over-priced prima donnas extravagant amounts when in most cases, they have no ability to manage their own money and become sitting ducks for dishonest agents and managers. This causes extremely high costs for fans, leaving them totally screwed.

CHAPTER 28
MINIMUM WAGES AND UNIONS.

It urinates me off when so many people who are uneducated, lazy, and uncaring in their jobs are shouting for a $15.00 minimum wage when they can't even make your lunch without screwing it up. Also, it is equally upsetting that left-leaning congressmen are using this issue to buy votes. They don't give a flip about senior citizens who worked all of their lives to make this country what it is. How about making the minimum Social Security payment equal to 15.00 an hour?

My next pet peeve is the uncaring and ineffective union representation in this country. There was a time when unions were necessary to protect workers from low pay and abuse, but in recent decades, unions have become a big money grab, getting their membership small pieces of candy while taking payoffs from major corporations and in many cases, being run by corrupt union bosses tied in some cases to organized crime.

I am a flight attendant with a major airline. One thing that we and pilots have been screwed on for decades is the fact that we do not get paid during boarding, deplaning and on ground-time between flights. These are extremely important and stressful times. We can be fired, fined by the FAA, and sued by passengers for any mistakes or even misunderstandings we may have. Amazingly, unions have never brought this to the forefront of negotiations. There is one major airline that has started giving crew members half of their pay rate during these times. Guess what. They do not have a union. Also, our top-out pay is 63.00 and change. This other airline has a top pay of more than 70.00 dollars per hour or trip. Again. No union.

Also, truck drivers have to wait around for hours with no pay and they are limited on hours they can drive and are saddled with many restrictions.

CHAPTER 29
DISCRIMINATION AGAINST FOLKS WITH A SOUTHERN ACCENT

I am a South Texas cowboy, and it totally urinates me off when northerners, easterners, westerners, and Hollywood writers brand southerners as being uneducated sub-humans who are automatically racist, sexist, homophobic, rednecks with violent tendencies.

In movies, most characters with a strong southern accent are depicted as idiots, racist bigots, or criminals. I.E. Sling Blade or The Green Mile. Screw Hollywood. I have conversed with businessmen, doctors, and professors who would not take me seriously because I had a southern drawl. To them, I say 'Stick It Where The Sun Don't Shine."

To me, nothing sounds more ignorant than these "perfect" speakers using terms like "Hella" or "Agro". When I'm around folks like that, I use as many of my Texisms as I can. I don't feel the need to impress them or anyone else.

My oncologist has a southern drawl. He's kept me alive for fourteen years longer than expected.

Dr. Red Duke was a medical pioneer who headed up the University of Texas Health Science Center for many years. I thought I had a drawl! OMG! Dr. Red was as Southern as they come. Another friend of mine, John F. Hamilton Jr., had a PhD in Electrical Engineering and Astro Physics. He was the head engineer for years in the Apollo missions. I don't claim to be brilliant, but I'm not an idiot, either. I've found in many cases, the ones with the education pedigrees are not always as smart as they would like for us to believe.

One of my dearest friends was Thurman T. Price. He worked for me in my barber shop as a shoe shine man. His parents and grandparents came out of slavery after the Civil War. He quit school in the 3rd grade to help his older brother shine shoes to help his mom feed his younger siblings after his father had died.

Thurman was never wealthy except when he pitched for the Kansas City Monarchs in the all-black baseball league. It was short-lived, though. Thurman was honest and hard-working and could only read a little bit because I taught him.

I first met him when I was in high school and worked part-time working cattle for the King Ranch. He was one of the black cowboys. Funny how he worked for me later. I've known many highly educated people, but I can honestly say that when he was alive, I would have chosen him to have my back ahead of pretty much any of the educated folks I've known.

Don't treat folks who speak differently from you as being less than intelligent because you have no idea what their education level is or what life experiences they've had.

In other words – don't be a pompous jerk.

Case in point – Any time you hear the word "redneck", you are made to believe that they are racist southerners. Redneck is a term that originally referred to farmers, ranchers, roofers, oilfield hands and carpenters because working outside would tend to make their necks red from sunburn.

It has nothing to do with race! As far as I'm concerned, all of the elitist anti-Southerner hypocrites can kiss my redneck ass!

CHAPTER 30
ILLEGAL IMMIGRATION

Oh my God! I am so urinated off at being dubbed a racist because I don't want the 4.2 million illegal aliens Buffoon Biden has invited to invade our country. Along with the 65 terrorist watch list folks who have been caught this year, I can't believe the left-wing liberals are okay with gigantic amounts of Fentanyl being smuggled by the illegals and the cartels.

Also, they don't care about the more than 3,000 illegals who have died by drowning or at the hands of coyotes and drug-dealing cartel thugs. They also don't give a tinker's damn about the border communities and land owners who have been inundated with illegals who, out of desperation or out of pure criminal intents, are breaking into homes and businesses, stealing all they can. Heaven forbid all these liberal sanctuary states and cities have illegals dropped at their doorstops!

Amazing how liberals brand DeSantis and Abbot as racists for bussing and flying illegals to these liberal sanctuary havens. Where was the outrage when Buffoon Biden was flying them out in the night and dumping them in red states under cover of darkness?

I am all for anyone coming to America for a better life if, and only if, they come legally like my grandparents did. If this makes me a racist, then I'll wear that stereotype. Hypocrites!

As I've said before, I am a flight attendant for a major airline, and we have them on our planes very often. Funny how they are given a cell phone, cash, clothes, supplies and a free ticket. They don't even have to show I.D. like I and every other real American is required to do.

The only other thing that urinates me off on this subject is that the idiotic republican party has never gotten behind true border security like Trump attempted to enact!

CHAPTER 31
TRANSGENDER ATHLETES

Okay, before you liberals lose your mind and call me a homophobe or bigot, let me say that I don't have anything against anyone in the LGBTQ community. I don't care what they do. I want them to do what makes them happy. They can be trans or have the total operation, but I don't want to pay for it for anyone, especially prisoners.

However, the thing that really urinates me off is when a male who has trained as a woman and competed as a man figures out that he'll never be good enough to win against males and conveniently becomes trans, calling himself a woman and compete in women's sports so that he can win medals.

Bull Shit! This is wrong on every point! I have one question – where in the hell is the feminist movement? Why are they not protecting real women? I know what is coming – in today's "Woke" society, he is a real woman. No f_cking way! Leftists that buy into this bullshit are neither considering the science nor the reality of this idiotic unfair practice.

If you want to have a trans league, more power to you, but stop punishing real women for accommodating the whims of folks who can never be a real woman.

Even with a sex change operation, that person's DNA is still male. Hate me all you want, because I don't give a damn!

CHAPTER 32
THE END OF MY BULLSHIT

In closing, I realize that I probably urinated off 75% of the folks who have read my book because only about 25%, by my estimation, can read all of this crap with an open mind and a sense of humor. However, just as I said in my preface, If my book offends your insecure, emotional sensibilities, I don't give a big rat's ass!

I love you all, no matter what!

Thanks for reading this turd of a book and making me rich.

I promise volume 2 will be much more fun.

God bless you, and God bless America!